Identity Theft Protection: Preventing Identity Theft in a Connected World

Discover Proactive Measures to Protect Your Identity and Stay One Step Ahead of Cybercriminals

By
Mark Derek Hamilton

D1738375

COPYRIGHT ©

DISCLAIMER AND LEGAL NOTICE

INTRODUCTION

Identity theft is becoming more of a problem in today's culture. With the increasing reliance on digital technology and the internet, our personal information is more vulnerable than ever before. As we go about our daily lives, we leave a digital footprint that can be exploited by identity thieves to commit fraud, steal our money, and damage our credit score.

Identity theft can happen to anyone, regardless of age, gender, or socioeconomic status. In fact, identity theft is one of the most common types of fraud in the United States, with over 4.4 million cases reported in 2020 alone. These cases resulted in losses totaling over $16.9 billion.

In this book, I will explore the many facets of identity theft prevention. Our aim is to provide a comprehensive guide for adults who are concerned about safeguarding their personal information and preventing identity theft. I will cover everything from basic preventative measures to advanced strategies for protecting your personal information.

The first section of the book will focus on the different types of identity theft, including credit card fraud, social security fraud, medical identity theft, and more. We will discuss how identity thieves obtain your personal information and the methods they use to commit fraud.

The second section of the book will cover practical tips and strategies for preventing identity theft. I will explore ways to secure your online accounts, recognize and avoid phishing scams, and protect your physical documents.

I will also dive into advanced techniques for protecting your personal information, such as using virtual private networks (VPNs), two-factor authentication, and password managers.

Throughout the book, I will provide real-world examples and case studies to help illustrate the importance of identity theft prevention. I will also offer step-by-step instructions and checklists to help you implement the strategies and techniques we discuss.

Without overwhelming you with technical jargon, I want to empower you with the knowledge and skills you need to safeguard your personal information and stay one step ahead of identity thieves.

If you're looking for a comprehensive guide on how to prevent identity theft, this book is for you. Whether you're a concerned citizen, a business owner, or simply someone who wants to protect their personal information, we are here to help. Let us work together to make the internet a safer and more secure place!

Identity theft is no longer uncommon. It spreads quickly and becomes a socioeconomic disaster. The fastest-rising economic crime is identity theft.

It is a crime in which a fraudster obtains critical pieces of your personal identity information, such as your social security number or driver's license, and utilizes it to their advantage. By going online, identity thieves can obtain a wealth of sensitive information about you. They begin by exploiting your personal identifying information, such as your social security number and name, as well as your credit card number or other financial account information. Once they have this information, they may rent an apartment, obtain a credit card, or generate a phone bill in your name.

Your personal information might be obtained by an identity thief at your mailbox or at home. Identity theft is terrible enough, but it is also a national industry at the present, relying mostly on tactics like diving. Identity theft and, as they improve, crackdowns are not where they should be. It's difficult to say since each law enforcement agency handles identity theft differently; this might involve credit card fraud, Internet fraud, or mail theft, among other things.

Detection Of Identity Theft and Credit Card Fraud

Monitoring and reporting credit is an important approach to uncovering fake accounts. Check your credit information on a regular basis, since there is a provision for free yearly reports from credit bureaus. Regularly check the websites of banks, credit card providers, and account issuers for frequent account activity.

The majority of identity theft victims are unaware they are victims until they are contacted by a debt collection agency about arrears they were unaware of, purchases they never made, or significant fees charged to their credit card account; or a lender tries to take back a car he did not know was his; or the police contact them after a crime has been committed in their name. It is critical to detect fraud as soon as possible in order to avoid damages and safeguard your credit rating. Inquire with your financial services provider about zero-liability assurances against fraud and particular resources to help you recover from your losses. If you have an account with them, certain banks will work with you. If you are a victim of identity theft, inform your financial service providers right away, check your accounts more often, and notify the three credit bureaus. (Equifax, Experian, or TransUnion). If someone uses your name, social security number, credit card number, or any other aspect of your personal information to apply for a credit card, make illicit transactions, access your bank accounts, or obtain credit in your name, this is considered identity theft.

Concerns About Social Security

For identification, use your social security number. Identity thieves exploit sensitive information such as social security numbers and driver's license numbers to get loans, products, and services.

Almost half of the students had their grades assigned based on their social security number. A person can obtain your social security number in a variety of ways, and most crooks begin with a phone book. They might collect government benefits using your name and social security number. They can also acquire a job using your social security number. Obtaining a new Social Security number may not solve your identity theft problems and may even exacerbate them. Even if your previous credit information is not linked to your new social security number, a lack of credit history under your new social security number might make obtaining credit difficult. Finally, there is no guarantee that a new Social Security number would not be misused by an identity thief.

Taking Action

Because each of these procedures requires you to give personal information, you run the danger of becoming a victim of identity theft.

According to the most recent data, the Better Business Bureau, CheckFree, Visa, and Wells Fargo have given consumers the following advice to protect themselves from financial identity fraud:

1. Prevent unauthorized access to your personal information.

2. Use the Internet instead of paper bills, bank statements, and checks. (paperless)

3. Think about using an electronic payment provider, such as your bank's or a billing website.

4. No longer send signed checks via mail.
Many of the most devastating examples, according to researchers, involve business insiders stealing sensitive personal information from corporate systems in order to examine people's portfolios. Contact a company's security or fraud department by phone. As your password, avoid using information that may be readily suggested or guessed, such as a string of numbers, phone numbers, the last four digits of your social security number, your date of birth, or your mother's maiden name.

Know how information is taken and what you can do to safeguard it, verify your personal information to discover problems promptly, and know what to do if you suspect your identity has been stolen. They might take your wallet or bag or persuade you to give them personal information. In a nutshell, any document containing personal information that you no longer require.

Putting Things Back Together

Identity fraud victims are spending more time settling cases, which has increased from 33 hours in 2003 to 40 hours in 2006. Most victims are not required to pay someone else's debt, but it is the time, worry, and many sleepless nights that you must spend to clean your file that truly damages most victims. It might take months, if not years, to repair the victim's reputation and the stressful path of ruin that is inflicting havoc.

Prevention is the most effective method.

Identity theft prevention is supposed to be a simple three-step process:

1. Restrict the use of social security numbers as a unique identifier for corporate reasons, a proposal proposed in Congress and repeatedly rejected over the last decade.

2. Make lenders need more identification and tighten credit card restrictions.

3. Limit credit bureaus, government and federal agencies, and marketing firms from selling personal information.

Identity theft prevention is not as complicated as it appears.

Personal recommendation: When using the Internet, employ technologies that strengthen your security and secrecy, such as digital signatures, data encryption, and "anonymity" services.

Identity theft is obviously a major nuisance for both the victim and the financial institutions who are duped by this activity. Identity theft is the fastest rising crime in the United States, according to the Federal Bureau of Investigations. It is believed to be worth $6 billion.

MAJOR IDENTITY THEFT COMPLAINTS AND HOW TO AVOID THEM

Identity theft is now one of the fastest-growing criminal offenses in the world. It tops the list as the number one consumer complaint in the United States, with about 35 people being victims of this heinous crime every minute. Sadly, the problem is likely to increase with the increasing use of the Internet.

Identity theft is a form of fraud that occurs when a person or a group of people steals your personal information for economic or social reasons. This happens in different ways. Thieves steal credit card payments and other outgoing mail from private mailboxes. They then change the address form on behalf of the victim to redirect emails and collect personal and financial information. They search in the trash can for canceled checks, bank and credit card statements and pre-approved credit card offers, hack computers to get your personal information, and steal information. They use malware to steal your information from the Internet. They also use email phishing to trick into providing them with your personal information. These are just a few of the more common ways of committing this crime. New tactics are constantly being introduced.

Although most of these crimes involve financial theft, there are many types of identity theft, ranging from driver's license theft to citizen service number theft. Statistics show that about 29% of identity theft affects credit or bank accounts. Here are the four most common types of identity theft complaints reported to the Federal Trade Commission:

1. Fraud With Government Documents And Benefits: This crime includes, for example, the theft of your social security number or driver's license, your Veteran's Administration benefits, or your tax refund check. Complaints in this category have kept on increasing year on year. The FTC has stated that tax or wage fraud has led to growth in this area. Tax returns, especially those with scheduled reimbursement, are new targets for criminals. Another system uses your social security number to allow illegal immigrants to work. This kind of fraudulent activity accounts for about 46%.

A CBS report in June of 2017 stated that 81 different people used a woman's social security number. The woman, who lived in San Francisco, California, heard nothing about it until she received an IRS tax return stating that she owed $15,813 in tax, even when she had not worked for several years. Ironically, these taxes are applied to work done in Texas.

2. Credit Card Fraud: It is responsible for up to 13% of identity theft. This can be done in several ways. Every time you give your card to a waiter, swipe at a gas station, or buy something online, you are exposed to this type of fraud.

A reported problem occurs at gas stations. The perpetrator installs a kind of shimmer on the pump that reads your credit or debit card information when you swipe your card for the gas purchase. Then they sell that information.

In January 2016, ABC News reported that two Mexican citizens were arrested at the Texas border after using information stolen from a Target credit and debit card security breach to purchase several thousand dollars. The Target breach is believed to affect 40 million credit and debit card accounts and the personal information of up to 70 million customers.

3. Phone And Utility Fraud: It accounts for 10%. Someone steals your personal information to use your name and credit to create an account with the electric or gas company, telephone company, or water company. These people steal your reputation and credit for their own benefit and even sell your information to third parties where hundreds of people can use it.

A crime like this also occurs on cell phones/mobile phone accounts and is expected to be the main complaint in this category.

4. Bank Fraud: 6%. This ranges from counterfeiting to issuing bad checks to electronic transfer of large amounts of money.

An article in the LA Times in January of 2017 published a story of a woman with five accounts compromised in three different banks.

A January 2018 report on the Wet Paint website said a former prisoner was charged with bank fraud after he opened a business account and deposited bad checks, stolen airline pension checks, and auto loans. He allegedly used his new business to access information from certain people in order to commit this fraud.

5. Others: It accounts for 25%. It covers every other category, including medical fraud and attempted fraud.

A press article published in 2018 reported that a young Marine had lost his wallet during a training camp in South Carolina. After the camp, he was stationed in California. Almost a year later, his mother called him and told him that he was wanted for a car robbery. He also owed more than $20,000 in medical expenses. It turned out that a man in South Carolina had used his driver's license to take a test drive and steal new cars.

The man also received medical treatment for injured hand and kidney stones surgery. Before the Marine could fix the problem, his check was garnished on the state's income tax return, and his credit rating was destroyed. He also had potential issues with his medical records. If he was visiting a family in South Carolina and needed medical help, his damaged medical records could impact the type of medical treatment he might receive.

Bureau of Justice Statistics had stated that identity theft cost Americans $24.7 billion in 2012 alone.

For many victims, the economic and psychological effects can be harmful and lasting. So what could you do to protect yourself from identity theft? Here are some tips to reduce your chances of falling victim to the crime:

- In order to ensure your protection against identity theft, never enter your social security number, credit or debit card number, unless you know the organization of the person requesting this information. Treat these details as confidential information.

- Avoid taking your social card and passport with you anywhere you go unless necessary.

- Keep this document as well as all-important authorities and insurance documents in a safe place

- Make sure never to print your social security number on your checks.

- Carry as little bank cards and credit cards as you can and regularly check that you still have them.

- Save all passwords in memory. Never write them down and never take them with you.

- Make your PIN-code and password difficult for others to guess. Do not use your date of birth, phone number, or the last four digits of your social security number as your password.

- If you are using an ATM, ensure no one is hovering over you and seeing that you are entering your password.

- Keep a list of your bank account and credit card numbers as well as phone numbers in a safe place. Do not provide financial information unless you know the organization or the person requesting it. Notify your bank or credit card company of suspicious phone requests such that it is requesting your account information.

- Always check your monthly financial accounts and credit card statements. If you see any unknown transactions, immediately notify your bank or credit card company.

- Immediately report lost credit and debit cards and checks. Your bank can immediately block outgoing money in your account.

- Instead of writing on the back of your credit card, write "See photo ID." This way, a thief who takes your car cannot make a big personal purchase without your ID card.

- Destroy all bank statements and financial requests before trashing them. If you don't want paper statements to be destroyed, then sign up for bank statements and online payments.

- Store outgoing mail in an official and secure mailbox.

- Install anti-spam and anti-virus software on your computer. Ensure you never open email any attachment from any individual you do not know. Be careful with pop-up windows on your computer. Sometimes you think you click to close it, but you passively accept some form of malware.

- Check your credit card file regularly and make sure the information is not incorrect. You are privileged to free credit reports from each of the three major credit bureaus (Equifax, Experian, and TransUnion) every year.

When utilized, these tips will provide proactive steps to avoid the financial and time hassle associated with identity theft. However, there is no complete failproof system that guarantees that you will never be a victim. The best advice you can offer is to get an identity theft protection plan. There are many companies that offer these plans. It is therefore advisable to carry out a comparative check before signing a contract with any particular company. Most plans include credit monitoring, monitoring of public records, and alerts to help with prevention. The major difference in an individual company's plans is when your identity is compromised. Some companies will send you a DIY kit, while others will give you advice over the phone. But, the best plans offer a full set of identity recovery, including investigators or agents trained to step in to help you do the hard work involved. In times of crisis, it would be a great advantage to have a professional lead your efforts to restore your identity.

Sadly, identity theft will be with us in the near future. Although the fear factor is high, it is good that we can take steps to protect ourselves and our families.

HOW TO AVOID BECOMING A VICTIM OF ONLINE IDENTITY THEFT

In the event that you want to apply for citizenship in a digital country and join the league of millions of other migrants on board to take advantage of the freedom and access to the wealth of information that the internet offers, you must first familiarize yourself with the web culture of getting used to the environment. If you don't, then you will stand out like a sore thumb that is very prone to being a victim of an online scam.

When you're ready, you'll enjoy the rest of your time in digital land, following a lighted path of other web surfers and avoiding the dark alleys often haunted by a reckless person.

The safety measures you take in the real world should also be replicated online. Whether it's buying something on eBay, paying your bills, or doing some online transactions because the risks and dangers of online theft are real. Adware, hacking, spyware, viruses, phishing (a method that tricks you into providing your personal information for identity theft), and mutations of these scams are a disturbing trend.

You might have received some of these mail scams in your email inbox or maybe on the internet as disguised eCommerce sites.

If you have been the victim of such scams and sabotages, you can testify that even the most discerning of you "never expected it". These covert operations chase you down when you least expect them and prove to inattentive skeptics that these threats are very real.

Anybody with limited knowledge of computer programs can take control of your computer. It's as easy as installing free remote control software on your PC and allowing voyeurism to take it over. Every movement you make is observed. The perpetrator can now steal your identity and send you spyware wrapped in an innocent-looking email disguised as a lost friend; after all, the person now knows a lot of things about you. In the worst-case scenario, they get you involved in one of their criminal activities. Believe it or not, I didn't get this from a Tom Clancy spy thriller. Just do a Google search on the word "identity theft" and you will see what result Google will bring to you. Over 150 million results will be returned—evidence of genuine concern and interest in this area.

So what could you do to protect yourself? You can actually do a lot. To begin with, use your common sense. Do not allow strangers to use your computer either in the office pr at your home. Don't throw your bank statements or payments in the trash, because it makes it easy picking for fraudsters.

When you are checking your emails, make sure not to click on any suspicious-looking attachments, even if it was sent from your mum.

Even if it is from a trusted colleague and the attachment is important, be sure to run it through updated antivirus software (make sure you get one) before you download it. Delete all suspected emails from anyone claiming to be a certain Prince of the Isle of Dr. Bunco, whose father just died and left him a billion-dollar inheritance, but because he needs a certain amount of money to release the inheritance, he now writes to you for aid (don't even ask how the certain Prince got your email), and as a reward for your help he is willing to share the legacy with you 70/30 to your benefit.

Get a firewall installed on your PC and set your browser's privacy settings to ensure a certain security level when browsing the Internet. Emails purporting to be from a particular banking or e-commerce site and indicating an overdue invoice or unpaid balance should always be treated with caution. If you are prompted to click this link and enter your personal information, do not do so.

Always launch a new browser, enter the organization's URL into your browser and decide if such a page is available and is similar to the one you got in your email. If you are still unsure, take the phone and call the organization. You have the right to know the truth about their organization. This brings me to what I really wanted to share with you; Ensuring you make a secure online transaction.

If you've been online for a while, you'll likely see how quickly and easily you can pay your bills online, how much you can shop at your favorite store, or just how to do a quick business transaction on sites like PayPal.

And as I mentioned above, phishers have so mastered the art of e-commerce site forgery that unsuspecting users are blindly lured in to reveal their personal information that they would normally never reveal to their husbands themselves.

This is what you need to do in order to protect yourself. Suppose you are buying from GAP. You have selected the product, and GAP will now take you to a page where you can enter your data. This is usually the first of four or five steps in an online shopping process. Now is the time to look for small but important details.

Two elements of your browser that are clearly recognized are the URL of the website you are on and the closed padlock. Make sure "http:" is now "https:" The padlock must also be closed. These two points are almost the first thing you should look for before giving your personal details.

However, these are not foolproof methods to check if a website is encrypted. The many authentication certificates available today allow phishers to easily obtain one and imitate the banking or e-commerce website. Terrifying, you will hardly be able to tell the difference.

Therefore, using the closed padlock as a measure to determine the authenticity of a website can sometimes be almost an illusion, but remains a necessary functionality for verification.

Some browsers also change the color of the address bar when browsing an encrypted website.

For instance, Firefox changes the color of the address bar from normal white to yellow when an encrypted website is displayed.

An alarm tone should sound when you are notified of an invalid or expired certificate. This clearly indicates that you must immediately stop all types of transactions.

Comodo, one of the largest certification bodies globally, offers a free download called "Verification Engine," which you can use to verify that the website you are visiting is reliable. I think this offers some security and is definitely worth downloading if you are not sure you can visit reliable sites.

Another precaution to make sure you are not being fooled is to visit PhishTank.com. PhishTank is a website that lives up to its name and an emergency room for information on phishing on the Internet. In addition to using the Comodo verification engine, you can have even more peace of mind by consulting the PhishTank Database. If you come across a phishing website, you can add it to the database. A site like PhishTank can only be kept up to date if users work together to spot these smelly phishers.

I hope you now have more confidence to face the dangers that the dark side of the Web can bring to you. If we educate ourselves and others on how to stop being victims and work together to make the internet safe, not only for ourselves but also for kids who are so much more vulnerable to fraud, we will then be able to truly make our living in the digital country a blissful one.

HOW TO AVOID BEING A VICTIM OF IDENTITY THEFT AT A FUEL STATION

I recently encountered some disturbing information when I stopped by my local supermarket. I arrived at the supermarket gas station late at night, jumped and pumped ten dollars worth of gasoline into my car, and walked in to pay my bill. I handed over my credit card and talked with the receptionist I visit several times a week because I don't like transferring large sums of money to powerful, money-hungry fuel grenades at the same time. After scanning my credit card, the front desk personnel gave me the receipt to sign and then indicated that he had my credit card number now.

Right there, I looked at the clerk in surprise and asked him to explain his comment. The employee reported my receipt, gave it to me, and showed me where the products I had purchased, the amount of my purchase, and the total sales were displayed. The receipt also included the type of card I used, my name, the credit card number with the first 12 numbers issued, the last four numbers printed clearly, the expiration date, type of transaction, and the approval number my card. The date and time of my transaction were at the end of the receipt. When I looked at this information, I asked how he could have my credit card number if it was not fully printed on the receipt. This comment gave the clerk a triumphant smile as he dived into his explanation.

The receptionist told me that each store is made to print and manually add all the credit card sales for the day to verify they are correct. The employee assigned to this task is kept for hours and adds the 5-mile long receipts. The clerk said each person's receipts contain the full credit card number, but not the cardholder's name on the receipt. The clerk waited patiently until I asked the obvious question, which I simply asked by saying how he could get my information if my name was not on my credit card number on the store copy.

The clerk explained how the 50km copy of the store contained the cardholder's full credit card number, as well as the total amount, date, and time of the transaction amount. Even if this information alone was not enough to pose a high risk, someone in combination with the copy of my receipt kept in the store would provide the person with enough ammunition to ruin my finances.

Customer Receipt:

1. Products Purchased

2. Amount of purchases

3. Total sales

4. Card type

5. Name of customer

6. The customer's credit card number, which only displays the last four digits.

7. Credit card expiration date

8. Date and time of purchase

Store's Receipt:

1. Customer's full credit card number

2. Total sales

3. Date and time of purchase

Match the customer's full credit card number and expiration date to the customer's name by matching the date, time, total sales, and the last four digits of the credit card number and bingo. The person has all the information they need on a long-awaited shopping trip.

To make matters worse, the clerk said the information is usually sent to their headquarters in a few days. Usually, this statement would please most people, and

I was initially relieved that my credit card information was not available indefinitely in stores until I ask how the information was sent to the head office. At first, I assumed that FedEx or a similar transportation service would bring the receipts to the head office. When I asked the clerk this question, I was told that the receipts had not been sent via a transport service, but returned to the head office by the milkman!

Now I do not have anything against the milkman. My family consumes their milk share every week, and I appreciate the milkman's thoroughness to make sure the store is always filled with fresh milk for my midnight trips. At the same time, I don't think the return of credit card receipts to the head office should be part of the milkman's duty. I mean, how secure our credit card information is during the cold trip to headquarters. Are receipts locked in a cabinet? Are they in an envelope in the passenger seat easily accessible to anyone passing by while the milkman goes to the supermarket freezer?

When asked these questions, the clerk said that he did not know how the receipts would be transported, but he did not think they were locked in a locker. I don't know anything about you, but I find this information disturbing. I wonder how secure our credit card information is when they drive in the milk cart in town. Is the envelope within reach of all who pass by, or is it at least hidden? Are the store copy of receipts goes along with the customers'? Or are customer receipts sent separately to the headoffice to provide poor security?

Even if customer receipts are sent out one by one, and even if the receipts are locked in a locker, I still wonder what a business could do with other customer information if they already manage sensitive customer information so carelessly.

This careless handling of customer information is not limited to convenience stores.

When I learned how my credit card information is processed in my local supermarket, I mentioned my new "awareness" to a friend who said that he previously worked for a popular electronics company that had customer's receipts immediately available in a locker in the back room of any employee who wanted to take a look.

This information, combined with the vulnerability of our information on the Web, makes it an insurmountable task to protect our information.

However, we can take steps to secure our information. We work very hard to secure and protect our credit card information and identity. We should not expect less from the places we often visit with our business.

IDENTITY THEFT AND PUBLIC WI-FI

In this chapter, it is my goal to explain to everyone how easy it is for anybody to see your personal and personal information and how it can harm you. Some people still think it doesn't happen often, but I can tell you that it happens more and more today, and I know from a friend whose identity was stolen that it can cause you a lot of grief and financial destruction for a long period of time.

First of all, I will explain to you how a computer uses the Internet in a network to describe its vulnerabilities. When you are on the Internet with Wi-Fi, your computer essentially communicates with your WiFi router by requesting a website or by transmitting and receiving information from the website. These transfers are called packets. Basically, your laptop sends a packet of information to the WiFi router. The router then sends a request through your Internet Service Provider to the website you are browsing on. The website then sends information back to your WLAN router and then back to your computer. You can see that everything goes through the WiFi router because it acts as a hub for all information with its own IP address for all computers and mobile devices connected.

Anyone who uses the same Wi-Fi network as you, either with password protection or not, will also be able to see everything in these data packets with a simple program that anyone can access from the Internet, also known as sniffing. Most of the information in these data packs is everything you do on the Internet. When someone sniffs your packs, they can see, read, or access emails, upload or download images, customer files, contracts, usernames, passwords, and credit card numbers. They are able to see everything. If they have your username and password, they can access the sites, and like many people have the same username and password for everything, they can gain complete access to everything you are doing. By the way, if you don't have a password manager yet, please get it. A password manager is a program that lets you store all of your passwords in one place. They are all encrypted and different, which minimizes the risk of losing all accounts due to hacking into one account. A free one that is good is KeePass; it works on all platforms and all devices.

If you are observant, you would have noticed that some websites have an http:// while some have https:// for the address. Https means that the website has a secure connection so that the data transferred between you and the website is encrypted and that when someone sniffs packets in your network, they cannot say what you are doing, which is good.

Note that many websites that use https have many vulnerabilities because they don't use them properly.

Browsers such as Internet Explorer, Mozilla Firefox, and Google Chrome use something called cookies. Cookies act like bread crumbs, so your browser leaves a trace of where you were. This facilitates faster returns and generally without reconnecting. That way, you can, for example, log in to Facebook, then close the browser, then open it again, go back to Facebook and not have to log in again. In the background, a cookie is placed in your browser, which indicates that you were there and that you have logged in. This means that your cookie bypasses the login interface.

This is also the reason why you suddenly see advertisements everywhere for a product that you have recently checked while you usually surf the Internet. Google has placed a cookie in your browser with which you viewed an article. If more Google ads appear, Google knows which ones will be sold to you.

These cookies are the reason why some websites that use secure https addresses are not totally secured because they do not use https to encrypt cookies, but the http address. This means that someone who sniffs your packages may not understand the information you exchange with the website, but may still be able to see cookies clearly. The sniffer can then take them and place them in their own browser to access everything you've just done.

All of this can be easily done on any network that you share with other users or home networks that have not set a password or have been hacked. Information theft is more common in open networks in places such as hotels, universities, schools, sports arenas, airports, cafes, buses, trains, work, restaurants, and wherever WiFi is freely available.

You can also remain unsafe if you are on your home network and do not have a password to join your network, or if the password is weak. Make sure your security is set to at least WPA encryption, WPA2 is even better. If you have WEP, it is time to change the router because this encryption is very weak and can be easily hacked. Another way to protect your own network is to disable your SSID transmissions. Have you ever noticed that when you are within a wireless network range, you see the message that says "so-and-so" is available that you can join the network? You can disable this option so that no one knows that your network is there, except those with an SSID.

Just think of it this manner. Anyone in the same cafe as you or someone who stays in a car near your office or home. He can just go to your email account, read everything, copy everything, send anything, take over your account, and gain access to your Facebook account. They can know all the details of your life, so it's easy to steal your identity, access your business files, and ruin your business! The possibilities are endless, and it's so easy for everyone to get involved, but at the same time, it's so easy to prevent it.

An easy solution is to use a VPN (Private Virtual Private Network) service. They are very easy to use these days and quite inexpensive. All you have to do is subscribe to a reputable VPN service and then download its simple software. Most business software works on all devices, including Android, iPhone, Apple. If you want to use the Internet in a place where you share WiFi or are not protected, start the application and connect to your VPN.

Once connected, you simply open the browser and usually do business without worrying about someone sniffing your packages and stealing your information. Setting up a VPN encrypts everything between you, then manages all the requests you want to make and returns the encrypted information. Private VPN mainly acts as an intermediary, so no one other than you knows that something is entering or leaving your computer.

Today, it is becoming more and more important to keep your information as secure as possible as more and more people want to steal. It is easier for the thief, particularly if he no longer needs to meet his victim physically.

PROTECTING YOURSELF FROM IDENTITY THEFT

Do you use email? Online payment? Do you look at your brokerage account online? Do you use a wireless network at home, at work, or on the go? Consider the following points to protect your personal and financial information.

Get The Latest Antivirus Software: Active and up-to-date antivirus software protects your computer from any virus threats. Most commercially available antivirus programs offer automatic weekly and emergency downloads of the latest updates. Scan all your virus files at least once a month. And for better protection, configure the antivirus program to scan all open files.

Get The Latest Anti-Spyware Software: Spyware running on your computer can collect private information such as your passwords and credit card numbers, display unwanted ads, and track your browsing habits. Spyware is usually hidden in an otherwise harmless program, often in shareware or freeware that you download on your computer. Make sure you know and trust the supplier of any software before downloading their free software. Some Internet Service Providers can help you find and remove spyware. The manufacturer of your antivirus software can also offer protection against spyware. Ensure you are protected from this growing threat.

Use A Firewall: Firewalls act as a protective barrier between your computer and the Internet and prevent unauthorized access to your computer while you are online. Make sure you have installed a firewall around your computer. Some ISPs offer firewall software to their customers, and you can purchase firewall hardware or software from your local computer store.

Regular Installation Of Security Updates: Many large software companies regularly publish updates or patches on their operating systems to close security vulnerabilities. On some websites, such as Apple and Microsoft, you can check your computer for missing updates. Check your computer for at least one time in a month for updates. For better protection, configure your computer to receive and install updates automatically when possible.

Protect Your Home Wireless Network: The default settings for most home wireless networks are not secure. Get in touch with your wireless software provider for information on how to enable encryption and improve the overall security of your home wireless network.

Be Cautious With Wireless Hotspots: Taking a few simple precautions when using wireless access points can protect your computer. Wireless technology is constantly evolving. Speak with the manufacturer of your network hardware to make sure you have the latest security technology.
Then install a firewall on all computers on the network, disable the wireless connection when you are not using it, use reliable encryption software, and disable the wireless display outside of Hoc mode. This allows only the wireless networks you create to use your wireless software. If you are not sure of the safety level of a wireless access point, do not use it to perform confidential tasks such as accessing email or personal financial information or for business.

Safeguard Your Passwords: Make your passwords as difficult to guess as you possibly can. Avoid obvious numbers and words like maiden name, date of birth, or birthday the people can easily guess. Never share your passwords with anyone, including relatives or friends.

Protect yourself against phishing scams: "phishing" is a email broadcast containing messages that falsely claim to be from a legitimate business. These messages often contain links to fake websites that ask you to provide personal information such as passwords, credit card information, social security numbers, or bank account numbers. Never provide personal information unless you are sure that the website is legitimate. You should also make sure that the website is encrypted.

Look out for the letter s at the end of the website address just before the beginning of the URL. This ensures that the website is running in safe mode.

How To Figure Out Phishing Emails: Phishing messages have considerably evolved over the past year and are often difficult to detect. The creators have now added realistic company logos and images, provided links to the real company's privacy policy, and even included a legal disclaimer at the bottom of the email. Ask yourself the following questions to determine if an email is part of a phishing scam:

Do I have any business relationship with this company? Should I expect this company to contact me in this manner and via this channel?

Should I expect this company to use this tone or make this request?

If you are not sure, call the company on the phone.

Never Open Unexpected Emails: You have to be careful with emails and attachments - even if they seem to belong to a friend - unless you expect them or if you are sure of what they contain.

Never Send Personal or Financial Information By Email: A lot of emails are not secured or encrypted and should not be trusted to send personal or financial information.

Protect Your Personal Information: Here are a few simple steps that could make a major difference. For instance, destroy confidential documents after use instead of throwing them away. Also, make sure you know who you're dealing with before providing any personal or financial information.
Do Not Use Your Social Security Number: Ask the organization and government authorities with which you transact business with to create customer number that you can use instead of using our social security number.

Check Your Financial Reports: Read all bank statements or credit card statements or correspondence upon receipt as soon as possible. Make sure that no changes or any transactions have been initiated without your consent and approval. If an invoice arrives abnormally late or doesn't come at all, call the company. Also, check your credit rating for inaccuracies.

Identity Theft Warning signs include:

1. Unauthorized debits or withdrawals

2. Not getting renewed credit cards, invoices or other emails

3. Getting credit cards that you did not request

4. Getting notification of changes you did not request

5. Being denied credit without obvious reasons.

While this may be a simple mistake on the part of the business, you should never just assume that it is a mere mistake that will be fixed. Follow-up with the company or service to know what the problem is.

If you believe that your personal data has been used unlawfully, you must immediately:

1. Review your credit reports

2. Put a fraud alert on your accounts

3. Close all open and/or fraudulent used accounts

4. Report a complaint to the Federal Trade Commission or the police.

PREVENTING CREDIT CARD IDENTITY THEFT

One of the biggest worries many people have is becoming a victim of identity theft. The majority of people just have the "Oh, this isn't happening to me" attitude. This is the wrong mindset for 1 in 5 people. Which of these five are you? The most common form of identity theft is credit card fraud, usually through completely taking over an account. With this type of crime, the thief has access to a credit card and simply starts shopping.

What makes this type of identity theft fraud is that the attacker often calls the bank or the credit card company and tries to find more information about the account holder with a means known as "fishing." Using this technology, which is old fashioned among private investigators, the perpetrator pretends to be an account holder and tries to change the account information, update the account for more credit, withdraw money, or manipulate it in another way. With enough information, many thieves can use one account to gain access to several others. With a debit card, you can access checks, savings, and even loan accounts through the bank.

Most banks and institutions have taken steps to prevent this customer account from being completely taken over. The best prevention, however, is to stop the thief before he can attack.

To do this, you need to follow these ten ways to avoid identity theft with a credit card. Most are simple, real security measures you are likely to take every day as part of your lifestyle. Others are just minor habits that you should practice to keep your account secure.

1. Carry Less Cards;

It sounds simple enough, but it's amazing how many people are walking around with six, seven, or more credit and debit cards in their pockets. It's an exaggeration and somewhat the same as wearing five pounds of gold and diamond jewelry. At some point, someone will decide to surprise you. The more cards you have with you, the easier it is for a thief to take your identity and fleece you for as much money as possible. Reduce the number of cards to two. Avoid using a bank debit card because they are the easiest to use to get money quickly and easily.

2. Be Watchful Of Your Card;

If you are using your card in a store or restaurant where it is given to an employee or a waiter, you should always keep an eye on the card. Never let the employee leave with your card and come back later. It is uncommon for people to think that these people can take advantage of their situation to copy card information or false swipe with a reader to collect the information for later retrieval.

3. Never Use A Debit Card Online;

Under no circumstance should you ever use a debit card linked to your bank account when shopping online.

Wherever you shop, debit cards are the main goal of thieves. Instead, use a closed account such as a prepaid card, a credit card, which is better protected. Companies like PayPal and others that offer separate cards from your checking account are popular options.

4. Keep A List Of Your Cards;

Keep a detailed list or a photocopy of every one of your cards. Know the account number, due date, phone number for reporting, etc. If your wallet is stolen, your home is burgled, or if you have lost one or more cards, this list can mean the difference between a few minutes to report a theft and a few hours while you find information and the perpetrator goes on to shop with your card accruing expenses on your card.

5. Keep Your Social Security Number Private;

Never give out your social insurance number or account number by phone or mail unless you are 100% sure that the person you are talking to and the business they claim to represent is legitimate. If you're not sure, don't spill it out. When a business calls you, assuming it is a utility company and prompts you for personally identifiable information. Ask them to call you back. Use the phone number in the phone book to make a call, not the number the person gave you on the phone. This confirms that the person is who they say they are and eliminates any possibility of "fishing."

6. Keep Your Receipts;

Keep the receipt when you make payment with a credit or debit card. Do not throw it in public trash or even in your home trash without first marking the account number or destroying the receipt. Most stores now only print the last four or five digits of your account to protect the information, but you only know if they did when you see that they did!

7. Don't Write Numbers On Checks

When you pay bills, NEVER put your credit card account number on a check when you pay the bill. If it gets into the wrong hands, the perpetrator will now have two options to take advantage of you (check plus card). Pre-printed checks with a driver's license are also a bad idea.

8. Check The Mail;

When a new card or check arrives, make sure you know when to wait for it and when to receive it. Even better, have them sent to a safe mailbox or the like.

9. Study Your Bank Statements;

Read your bank statements carefully, and each time they reach you. Some thieves steal a card number, use it one time and discard it. This leads to a much lower chance of being caught. Most scammers are not even noticed because account holders often just look at the "Total Due" line in the account and don't read the lines.

10. Order a Credit Report;
Request for your credit report every year from the three agencies. By law, they must provide you a free annual report. So use that. Read it and make sure that there are no accounts payable that you do not know of and no claims in your file that you have not approved, etc.

I believe these ten ways to prevent identity theft will help protect you and your finance. These are simple things that require a little effort on your part, but which can greatly reduce your chances of being targeted for identity theft.

WHAT TO DO IF YOU ARE THE VICTIM OF IDENTITY THEFT

You have to take action to respond to identity theft in order for you to fix it as soon as it is suspected. What steps should I take if I am a victim of identity theft?

If you fall victim to identity theft, take the following four steps as quickly as possible and keep a detailed note of your conversations and copies of all correspondence.

1. Place a fraud alert on all your credit reports and access your credit reports. Fraud alerts will prevent an identity thief from opening additional accounts using your name. In order to place a fraud alert on your credit report, contact the toll-free fraud number of one of the three consumer reporting companies below. If you do not receive a confirmation from the company, please contact the company directly.

Equifax: 1-800-525 6285; [http://www.equifax.com;] P.O. Box 105069, Atlanta, GA 30348-5069
Go to the Equifax website to place a fraud alert.
https://www.equifax.com/personal/credit-report-services/credit-fraud-alerts/

=========================

Experian: 1-888-EXPERIAN (397-3742);
[http://www.experian.com;] P.O. Box9532, Allen, TX
75013
Go to the Experian website to place a fraud alert.
https://www.experian.com/ncaconline/fraudalert

===========================

TransUnion: 1-800-680-7289;
[http://www.transunion.com;] Anti-fraud division,
P.O. Box 6790,
Fullerton, California 92834-6790
To go TransUnion website, place a fraud alert.
https://fraud.transunion.com/fa/fraudAlert/landingP
age.jsp

===========================
Once you have ordered a fraud alert on your report,
you have the right to order a free copy of your credit
report from any of the three consumer reporting
companies. When you have your credit reports sent to
you, be sure to review them carefully. Look for
inquiries from businesses you haven't contacted,
accounts you haven't opened, and debts on your
accounts that you do not know about. Check out for
information such as your social security number,
address(es), name or initials, and employer and make
sure they are correct. If you find any incorrect,
fraudulent, or suspicious information, request to have
them removed.

When correcting your credit report, be sure to make
use of an identity theft report with a cover letter that
explains your request for the fastest, most
comprehensive results. Then check your credit reports
regularly.

2. Close accounts that you believe or are sure have been tampered with or opened fraudulently.
Place a call to and talk to someone in a company's fraud or security department. Do a thorough follow up and attach copies (NOT originals) of receipts. It is imperative to inform your credit card companies and banks in writing. Send your letters through a registered mail with the requested receipt so that you can document what the business received and when. Save a file with your correspondence and attachments.

Use new personal identification numbers (PINs) and passwords when opening new accounts. Do not use easily accessible information such as the last four digits of your social security or phone number, or a series of consecutive numbers, mother's maiden name, date of birth.

If the identity thief has carried out any debit or credit transaction on your accounts or opened accounts fraudulently, ask the company for forms to dispute these transactions:

Ask the representative to send you the company's fraud dispute forms in case of any debits and charges on existing accounts.

In the event that the company does not have special forms, use the sample letter to dispute the fraudulent charge. In either case, write to the company at the address provided for "Billing Requests," NOT the address used to send your payments.

* For new unauthorized accounts, you can either file a dispute immediately to the company or report it to the police and give the company a copy called the "Identity Theft Report."
If you are making a dispute directly with the company and you don't want to report it to the police, ask if the company will accept FTC Identity Theft Report. Otherwise, ask the company's representative to send you their anti-fraud form.

But if you submit a report to the police and then submit an identity theft report to the company, you get more protection. In the event that the company has already listed these fraudulent accounts or liabilities on your credit report, they would stop reporting these fraudulent accounts if you report identity theft information. Use the cover letter to explain your rights to the company by making use of the Identity Theft Report.

When you have resolved your identity theft dispute with the company, request for a letter from the company stating that they have closed down the disputed accounts and cleared off the fraudulent debts, this letter is your best proof in the event that any error relating to this account reoccur in your credit report or if you are contacted again regarding the fraudulent debts.

3. Submit a complaint to the Federal Trade Commission, which you can do with the FTC's online complaint form; or by calling the FTC's toll-free Identity Theft Hotline: 1-877-ID-THEFT(438-4338); TTY: 1-866-653-4261; or write to Identity Theft Clearinghouse, Federal Trade Commission, 600 Pennsylvania Avenue, NW, Washington, DC 20580. Do not forget to call the hotline to update your complaint if there is any additional information or concerns.

By reporting your identity theft complaint to the FTC, you are providing important information that law enforcement agencies across the country can use to track down and arrest identity thieves. FTC has the ability to refer to identity theft victims' complaints to other government authorities and companies for more action and can act and investigate companies for violating agency laws.

Also, you can give the police a hard copy of your online complaint form you must have printed, which must be included in their police report. The FTC's printed identity theft complaint may, in addition to the police report, constitute an identity theft report and qualify for certain safeguards.

This identity theft report can be used to;

i. Permanently prevent false information from your credit report.

ii. Prevent debts from reoccurring in your credit report.

iii. Prevent a business from continuing to collect debts due to identity theft.

iv. Include a full fraud alert on your credit report.

4. Report it to your local police department or the police in the community where the identity theft occurred.

Call your local police station and let them know you want to report your identity theft. Ask them if you can submit the report in person. If you can't, ask if you can submit a report over the internet or on the telephone.

For more information on automated reports, see below.
If the police are not ready to take your report, tell them you want to file for a "Miscellaneous Incident" or try another jurisdiction such as your State Police Department.

You can also check with the Attorney General's office in your state to see if state law requires police to report identity theft. Look up the phone number on the Blue Pages of your phone book or visit http://www.naag.org for a list of attorneys general.

When you visit your local law enforcement agency to file your report, bring a hard copy of your FTC identity theft complaint, personal cover letter, and other supporting documents. Cover letters are meant to explain why a police report and an identity theft complaint are so important to the victim.

HOW THE LEGAL SYSTEM CAN ASSIST YOU IN THE EVENT OF IDENTITY THEFT

It wasn't that long ago that people weren't so worried when they lost a credit card or threw away a bill. They knew they could contact their creditors and resolve the issue fairly quickly. But today, you may be a victim of identity theft without you being aware of it. This harmful crime is also difficult to prosecute, as it is difficult to track down and identify the criminal.

A few years ago, the US House Ways and Means Committee released a report with startling statistics on identity theft. They estimate that over a period of 10 years, approximately 57 million Americans were victims of identity theft. Half of them have no clue how the thief obtained their personal information, although a quarter knew that the identity theft was a result of a stolen or lost checkbook, credit card, personal mail, or social security. Some victims have even reported that the identity thief used his personal information to commit a crime under false identities.

In 2015, the Federal Trade Commission announced that reports of identity theft were up 33% from the same period the year before. In 2015, they were aware of over 800,000 cases of identity theft. The states with the most reported cases of identity theft were Texas, Florida, Arizona, Nevada, and California.

And nearly three-quarters of reported fraud cases involved the use of the personal information of the victim for the purposes of utility, banking fraud, credit card, or phone. They also found that the misuse of victims' personal information lasted for an average of between three to six months, resulting in a total loss of around $5billion to victims and over 300 million hours spent resolving the issue.

The 2015 FTC investigation found over $50 billion in business losses due to identity theft. They also reported that each victim that year has spent between $500 to $1,200 and 30 to 60 personal hours to resolve their credit issues. Sadly, we can hope that this trend will weaken in the near future. Identity theft appears to be easier, not more difficult, as criminals learn to hide their crimes from victims for longer and hide from law enforcement longer.

Sadly, there is not a single database of identity theft cases in the United States, and the Commission suspects that the number of crimes is severely underreported. The classification of these crimes as identity theft varies from one state to another state and from one police department to the other. The 2015 survey showed that 60% of identity theft victims did not report it to the police! Only one out of five had even reported the problem to their credit bureau.

Identity theft is currently the subject of a federal investigation by federal agencies such as the FBI and the Secret Service.

The Department of Justice usually deals with cases through a local US Attorney's office. In 2014, US Attorneys said they filed more than 2,000 cases of identity theft across the country (compared to the 9 million victims every year). That year, the Secret Service arrested more than 3,000 people, and the average actual loss of damage in closed cases was over $46,000 each. The FBI also reported 1,425 convictions for identity theft, and over 1,000 of these cases are for bank fraud. In 2014, the Postal Inspectorate arrested just over 1,700 people. Even the IRS reported real and suspected cases of identity theft in questionable tax returns in 2014 and estimated that they had received around 150,000 fraudulent returns and claims of over $750 million. Today, the federal government recognizes that identity theft is the fastest-growing financial crime in the country.

One reason for the seemingly low number of identity theft charges and convictions is the government's incapability to define specific crimes. In 1998, Congress passed the first identity theft act, the Identity Theft and Adoption Deterrence Act, designating identity theft as a federal crime and making prosecution of the criminals a little easier.

The law mandated the Federal Trade Commission to receive complaints and conduct public awareness on identity theft.

The Identity Theft Penalty Enhancement Act of 2004 provided penalties for aggravated identity theft, including cases where identity theft was used to commit more serious crimes.

The Fair and Accurate Credit Transactions Act of 2003 amended the Fair Credit Reports Act to address identity theft and related consumer issues, allowing victims to work with credit bureaus and creditors to remove implicating information caused by identity theft from customer's credit reports. The Internet False Identification Act of 2000 amended the old False Identification Crime Control Act of 1982 to cover online crimes with false identities. Violators can be fined and/or jailed for sending or producing false identification.

Private individuals are encouraged to take proactive steps to detect and/or prevent identity theft. Obviously, it is much less stressful to prevent this from happening than to try to solve problems after the crime has been committed.